Social Studies Made Simple

Grade 1

Written by Beth Alley Wise

FS-23221 Social Studies Made Simple Grade 1
All rights reserved—Printed in the U.S.A.
Copyright © 1997 Frank Schaffer Publications
23740 Hawthorne Blvd.
Torrance, CA 90505

D1516434

Introduction

First-grade students move from the security of their homes and families into the school community. Social Studies helps them make connections to the larger world. They will have many questions.

What are other families like?

How did our country start?

How are other places different from where we live?

How can I learn more about others?

Frank Schaffer's Grade 1 *Social Studies Made Simple* is divided into several sections—history, cultures, national identity, geography, economics, civics and citizenship, communication, and transportation—each with a set of reproducible pages for your students to use along with specific activities, projects, and ideas. These relevant activities are solidly linked to the full curriculum including links to language arts, mathematics, science, and the expressive arts. This program provides young learners with exciting projects and intriguing hands-on activities designed to help them gain the knowledge, skills, and civic values necessary to become active and reflective citizens.

One of the goals of the Frank Schaffer *Social Studies Made Simple* program is to make learning fun for first-graders. The activities engage students minds, appeal to their innate curiosity, and give them opportunities to express their creativity.

The activities in *Social Studies Made Simple* address a variety of learning styles so that each student will find activities that allow him or her to do well. The end product will be students who find the classroom to be a challenging and rewarding environment for learning.

FS-23221 Social Studies Made Simple ▪ © Frank Schaffer Publications, Inc.

Social Studies

Studying Social Studies can open children's eyes to the world around them using the arts, music, history, geography, and other cultural disciplines.

CONCEPTS

- United States history is linked to the history of families.
- Culture describes the language, art forms, foods, and lifeways of different peoples.
- The United States developed its identity from the ideals and contributions of its people.
- The land, climate, and population of the United States affects who we are and how we live.
- Our lives are affected by our work and how we trade with others.
- We all have responsibilities as citizens.
- Communication and transportation link us to the rest of the world.

RESOURCES

Books

Charlie Needs a Cloak by Tomie dePaola. Prentice-Hall, New Jersey, 1974.

Loving by Ann Morris. Lothrop, Lee & Shepard, New York, 1990.

When I Was Young in the Mountain by Cynthia Rylant. E. P. Dutton, New York, 1982.

As the Crow Flies: A Book of Maps by Gail Hartman. Bradbury Press, New York, 1991.

The Story of the Statue of Liberty by Betsy Maestro and Giulio Maestro. Lothrop, Lee & Shepard, New York, 1986.

The Flag of the United States by Dennis Fradin. Children's Press, Chicago, Illinois, 1988.

Katy and the Big Snow by Virginia Lee Burton. Houghton Mifflin, Massachusetts, 1971.

This Is the Way We Go to School: A Book About Children Around the World by Edith Baer. Scholastic, Inc., New York, 1990.

One Minute Stories of Great Americans by Shari Lewis. Doubleday, 1990.

All Kinds of Families by Norma Simon. Whitman & Co., 1975.

My Perfect Neighborhood by Leah Komaiko. Harper & Row, 1990.

Videos, Films, Filmstrips, Slides

Families Are Alike and Different. A 12-minute film or video #HP-5964C. Coronet Films & Video, Deerfield, Illinois, 60015.

America, My Country. A 10-minute film #HP-1939. Coronet Films & Video, Deerfield, Illinois, 60015.

Homes and Neighborhoods. Six 8-minute filmstrips with accompanying cassettes #BR20412-ASBTG. Society for Visual Education, Inc., Chicago, Illinois, 60614.

Presidents' Day. A 10-minute video #WUL8030C. Charles Clark Co., Inc., Bohemia, New York, 11716.

Computer Software

Sticky Town Bear. Society for Visual Education, Inc., Chicago, Illinois, 60614.

Family Histories

A family is a group of people who love each other and who work together to take care of each other. Some families are small. They may have only two people. Some families are big. Big families may have a mother, father, brothers, sisters, aunts, uncles, grandmothers, grandfathers, and other people who are related. Invite students to describe their families and how they take care of each other.

FAMILY FOCUS

Class Activity

Encourage students to ask grandparents or other older relatives to share stories about their experiences when they were children. Students should ask the older adults to describe the houses they lived in and the things they liked to do. Have students look at old pictures of their families, too. They may want to organize and display the stories and photographs in a scrapbook where they can be revisited, shared, and added to.

MAKE A FAMILY TREE

Class Activity

Making a family tree is a fun way to show all the members of a family. Interested students may want to make a tree for their families. Remind them that while some family members may no longer be alive, they should include them. It will help them see how each of their families has changed.

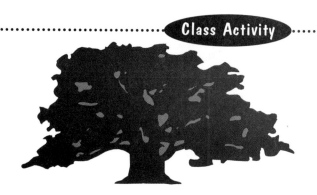

Invite each student to paint a big tree on poster board. As the paintings dry, copy reproducible page 2 and distribute two or three copies to each student. Then have students cut out an acorn for each person in their families. Help students write the name of a family member on each acorn with a title on the top of the acorn to tell how the person is related to them. When the paint is dry, have students glue the acorns on their trees. You may want to suggest to them that they place the names of the oldest relatives near the top of the tree and the youngest relatives at the bottom.

Name _____

My Family Tree

Color and cut out the acorns. Listen as your teacher tells you how to use the acorns to make your family tree.

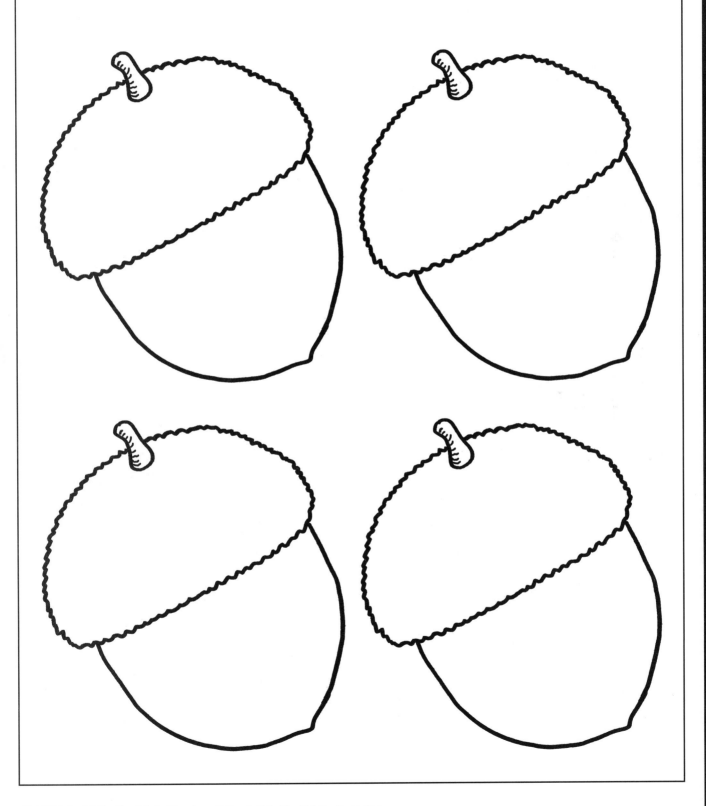

Change

In this unit, students will look at how change affects their lives.

CHANGES, CHANGES

Class Activity

Ask students to bring in photographs of family members at various stages of their lives—births, their first days of school, high school graduations, marriages, and so on. Point out that change is something that we all experience—young and old alike. Ask students to discuss changes that have occurred in their lives. Then have them draw illustrations of these changes.

TIMES ARE A CHANGIN'

Class Activity

Students can take the roles of Time Detectives to solve the mysteries behind changes in your community, such as why a favorite swimming area is no longer open for swimming or why a playground is being converted to a different use. Time Detectives may wish to interview several people to find the answers. Encourage students to use Who? What? When? Where? and Why? questions as they investigate.

Possible Interview Questions:
- *Who is responsible for throwing garbage in the lot near our school?*
- *What caused our local river to become polluted?*
- *When was our school built?*
- *Where was our community's first police station built?*
- *Why did our parents move to this community?*

MAKE A CHANGE FOR THE BETTER

Class Activity

Plan a change around the school that will make the school nicer. For example, you may decide to paint the garbage cans or plant some flowers. Invite other classes to add their special touches to this project.

A STORY FROM LONG AGO

Class Activity

Invite community historians or older family members to share stories and pictures of interesting events that happened in your community long ago. Then have small groups work together to write newspaper headlines to record their favorite event. You may want to begin by pointing out headlines used in your local newspaper(s). Reproduce page 4 for students to use as a guide for this activity.

An Important Event

Draw a picture of an event from the history of your family or your community. Write a headline for the event and add the date when it happened.

(Headline)

(Date)

Old Ways, New Ways

Over time, people have changed the ways they do things. Share some of the following examples of changes that made work easier, faster, or more fun.

ROLLER COASTERS

Class Activity

Have students ask older family members to describe the roller coasters they rode as children. In what ways are new roller coasters like the old models? In what ways are they different? Explain that the first roller coasters, built long ago, were wooden slides covered with ice. Students sat on sleds to make the bumpy ride. Invite students to build a miniature model of a new roller coaster using blocks, plastic building pieces with connectors, toy wagons or carts, and other available construction materials.

TALLY STICK

Class Activity

Point out to students that some people long ago used tally sticks to count things. If a herder wanted to keep track of the number of sheep in his or her herd, for example, he or she would make a notch in the stick for every sheep. Invite students to make a tally stick from a cardboard tube. Have them mark circular "notches" with crayon. Have them discover the disadvantages of such a system as they keep count of objects, time, or people for an entire day.

QUILL PENS

Class Activity

Explain that a quill is a pen made from a feather. The quill had to be dipped in ink before writing. Brainstorm other types of writing instruments. Then distribute copies of reproducible page 6. Provide feathers and ink (or grape juice) for students to complete the activity.

FS-23221 Social Studies Made Simple ▪ © Frank Schaffer Publications, Inc.

Feather Fun

Use a feather and ink to sign your name.

Draw something old used for writing.	Draw something new used for writing.

Our Country's History

NATIVE AMERICANS

Class Activity

Remind students that the first people to live in the land that we now call the United States were Native Americans. Many different Native American groups or tribes had different ways of life. Some tribes made tipis from animal hides and painted symbols on their tipis. The symbols told a story.

Write the message at the right on the board and let students "read" it. Then set out brown paper bags. Ask students to write a sentence or two on the bag about things they think Native American students may have done long ago using symbols. Students may enjoy wrapping the paper around three sticks to make a tipi model.

PILGRIMS

Class Activity

Teach students to play a version of stool ball, a game that Pilgrim children may have played on the Mayflower on their long journey to America.

How to Play:
- *Form two teams.*
- *One team lines up facing a stool. Players roll a kickball, trying to hit the stool.*
- *The other team tries to keep the ball from hitting the stool by catching it and rolling it back.*
- *A point is scored each time the ball hits the stool. After three hits, the teams change positions and play begins again. The first team to score 21 points wins.*

COLUMBUS

Class Activity

Explain that when Christopher Columbus reached America, he thought he had arrived in Asia. Have students trace his path from Spain to the Caribbean on a globe. Let them suggest reasons why they think Columbus and his crew got lost on their historic voyage.

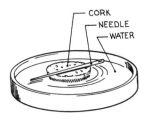

Invite students to make a compass, a simple tool that Columbus could have used to find his way. You will need one small bowl of water, one magnet, one sewing needle, and one cork. Instruct students to place the cork in the water. Then have them rub the magnet over the needle 50 times in the same direction. Lay the needle on top of the cork. Watch the cork turn. The needle will always come to rest pointing north. Use the compass to locate objects in the north end and the south end of the room.

SPOTLIGHT

Class Activity

Distribute copies of reproducible page 8. Invite students to learn more about their country's history by looking at monuments built to remember famous American presidents.

Spotlight: National Monuments

These are symbols of our country.

George Washington was the first president of the United States. This monument was built to honor George Washington. You would have to climb 897 steps to get to the top!

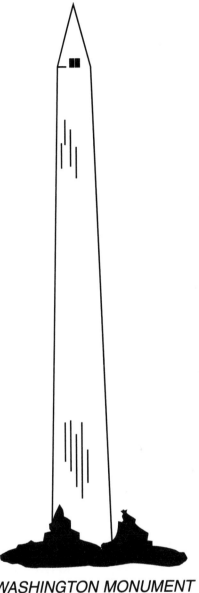

WASHINGTON MONUMENT

LINCOLN MEMORIAL

Abraham Lincoln was a president of the United States. This monument was built in honor of Abraham Lincoln. A picture of the Lincoln Memorial is on the back of a penny.

Families From Other Lands

Reinforce the idea that families come from all over the world to live in the United States. Remind students that each family has its own special activities and customs.

EATING UTENSILS

Class Activity

In advance, prepare a large serving of Chinese noodles. Distribute chopsticks to students and explain that people in Asia eat with chopsticks. Teach students the Chinese word for chopsticks, *kuai-zi.* Then let them have fun as they try using the wooden utensils to serve and eat the noodles.

HEAD WEAR

Class Activity

Explain that some families wear traditional clothing from the country where their relatives once lived. Many African-Americans wear scarves tied around their heads. Cut long rectangles of brightly colored cloth. Let students wrap the cloth around and around their heads, turban-style, tucking the ends at the back to create an African-style head covering.

LET'S CELEBRATE!

Class Activity

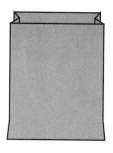

Tell students that families have their own special ways and reasons for celebrating. Students may decorate the classroom for a celebration such as Cinco de Mayo, Los Posadas, or for a classmate's birthday by hanging colorful streamers and a piñata. Stuff a large paper bag with goodies and newspaper before pinching and tying the top closed. Cover the bag by gluing crepe paper in place. Then hang the piñata and let students take turns hitting it with a stick until it spills open, scattering the goodies.

TANGRAM PUZZLE

Class Activity

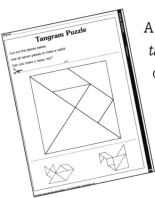

A favorite pastime in some cultures is to create animals with geometric shapes called *tangrams.* Distribute copies of the tangram pieces on page 10. Invite students to cut out the pieces and arrange them to make a swan, a rabbit, and other animals.

FS-23221 Social Studies Made Simple ▪ © Frank Schaffer Publications, Inc.

Tangram Puzzle

Cut out the pieces below.

Use all seven pieces to make a rabbit.

Can you make a swan, too?

 ··· CUT ···

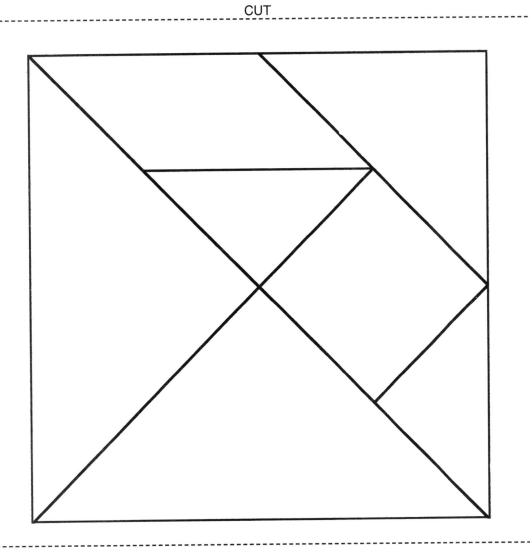

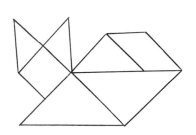

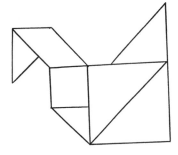

FS-23221 Social Studies Made Simple ▪ © Frank Schaffer Publications, Inc.

Native Tongue

HELLO! HELLO!

Take a poll to find out which languages, other than English, are spoken by students in your classroom or their family members. Encourage students to say "hello" in the other languages. Make a chart showing the words for *hello* as well as other phrases such as "How are you?" in each language.

Say Hello!			
Guten Tag	German	*Ave*	Italian
Bonjour	French	*Hola*	Spanish
	Konnichi wa	Japanese	

GREETINGS!

Explain that most people in America greet friends by smiling, saying hello, or waving. Have students discuss other ways to greet people. Then encourage pairs of students to act out gestures of greeting that might be used in the following situations.

- *Greeting your mother or grandmother.*
- *Welcoming your favorite sports team.*
- *A soldier greeting the president.*
- *A baseball player greeting a team member who has just hit a home run.*
- *A husband greeting his wife.*

I FOUND IT!

Distribute copies of page 12. Explain that some signs are used and understood by people all over the world. Ask students to look at each sign and write the name for the object or service they would find where the sign was posted. As a further challenge, have students think of a place they would want to find on a trip, such as an amusement park, swimming area, or hiking trail, and create a sign for it.

FS-23221 Social Studies Made Simple ▪ © Frank Schaffer Publications, Inc.

Name _____

I Found It!

Look at the signs. What can you find at each place? Write the word.

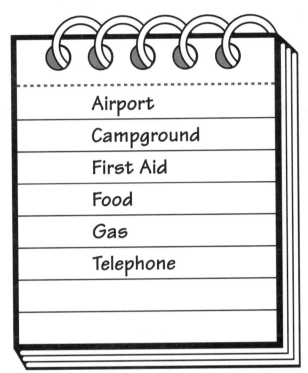

Airport

Campground

First Aid

Food

Gas

Telephone

_____

_____

_____

_____

_____

_____

 **Try This!** Think of a new sign. Draw it on the back of this page.

Let's Celebrate!

CHART IT!

Class Activity

Display a pocket chart with the heading "Let's Celebrate!" Poll students to discover their four favorite holidays. Place the names of those holidays on the chart as indicated below. Then on 5" × 7" index cards, ask students to draw pictures of how their families celebrate each holiday. Have students share their favorite memories or traditions as they place their cards in the chart.

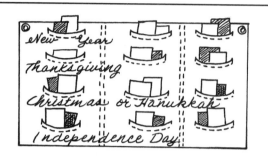

Let's Celebrate!

New Year

Thanksgiving

Christmas or Hanukkah

Independence Day

NEW YEAR'S DAY

Class Activity

Have students organize a New Year's Eve celebration regardless of the time of year! Help them choose and research traditions from several cultures to include in their celebration.

- *Chinese people often celebrate the New Year with a dragon dance.*
- *Many people bring in the New Year with lots of noise: bells, sirens, shouting, party blowers, horns, fireworks, and such.*
- *Students in Belgium write notes to their parents.*
- *The Chinese end their New Year's activities with a Lantern Festival.*

AMERICA ON PARADE

Group Activity

Organize a parade to celebrate all of the holidays. Students can organize themselves into cooperative work groups. Each group should select a holiday and plan a variety of parade activities that tell about it. Some of the activities might include creative floats on wagons, informative banners, colorful costumes, humorous sandwich boards, lively bands, decorative masks, and high-stepping dancers. Invite other classes to gather along the parade route to learn more about holidays in America.

MASK MAKER

Class Activity

Discuss with students celebrations they know about where masks might be worn, such as Halloween, Chinese New Year, Mardi Gras, Brazilian Carnival, and Kwanzaa. Distribute copies of the mask outline on page 14 and let students create bright, festive masks.

FS-23221 Social Studies Made Simple ■ © Frank Schaffer Publications, Inc.

Name _____

Mask Maker

Color and cut out the mask.

Staple yarn to each X.

Decorate the mask with feathers, beads, or other things.

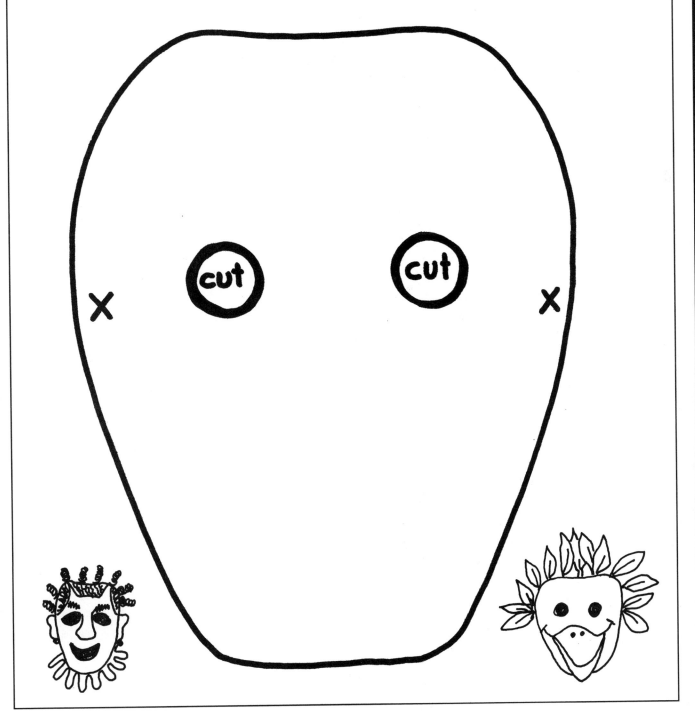

Toys and Games

Further explore cultures by playing games that are popular with students in other countries.

CATCH THE DRAGON'S TAIL

Tell students that Chinese celebrations and games often involve dragons. Invite students to join in this fun game which features the friendly beast.

How to Play Catch the Dragon's Tail

- Form "dragons" by having groups of students line up one behind the other with their hands on the shoulders of the person in front of them.
- At a signal, the head of the dragon (the first person in line) tries to catch the tail (the last person in line).
- If the head catches the tail without breaking the line, the dragon wins. If the line breaks, or if the tail is caught, a new head is chosen before play continues.

HOPSCOTCH

Explain that in Hopscotch, players toss a pebble and then hop from one section to another, skipping the block where the pebble landed. Use some of the Hopscotch boards shown here to play the game. Then challenge students to invent their own version of Hopscotch with either a twist to the old rules or a new design for the board.

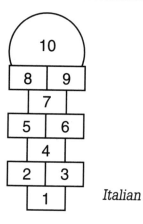

American

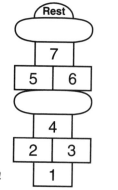

Italian

3	4
2	5
1	6

English

SHADOW TAG

Ask students to share tag games they have played. Explain that tag games are popular all over the world. One version of tag called "Shadow Tag" is played by students in sunny countries such as Saudi Arabia. To play the game, choose one player to be "IT." Explain that the object of the game is for "IT" to step on the shadows of the other players. If he or she is successful, the other player becomes "IT," but must count to 10 before play continues.

ALQUERQUE

Reproduce Alquerque (ahl-CARE-kay) game boards on page 16. Each pair of students will need a game board and two sets of 12 similarly-colored buttons to play the game. Read the rules for this Spanish game together before students begin play.

FS-23221 *Social Studies Made Simple* ▪ © Frank Schaffer Publications, Inc.

Alquerque— A Game From Spain

How to Play

Move buttons along the lines.

Move one space at a time.

If you "jump" your friend's button, take it off the board.

The person with the last button on the board wins!

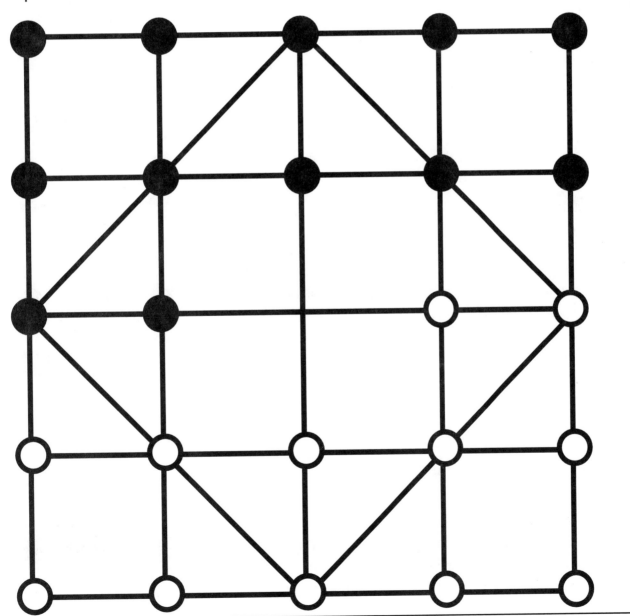

Art in Many Cultures

Art Project

*S*andpainting

Students will enjoy this art activity that is a favorite with the Navajo. In advance, mix sand and powdered tempera in plastic squeeze bottles. When you are ready to begin, have students draw a design on cardboard with pencil or crayon. Instruct them to cover one section of the design at a time with glue and then squeeze colored sand over the glued area. Repeat this for each section of the design until it is completely painted with sand.

CLAY POTTERY

Class Activity

Show examples of pottery dishes and utensils. Explain that people in all parts of the world use clay found near their homes to make tools, cooking utensils, dishes, jewelry, and ornaments. If possible, invite a local potter to demonstrate his or her craft and assist the students while they explore this medium or set out potter's clay and let students experiment with different techniques to make their own works of art. You may wish to demonstrate techniques for making coiled pottery, slab pottery, and pinched pottery.

ORIGAMI

Class Activity

Teach students the ancient Japanese art of paper folding. Tell them that origami was first used on gifts as a good luck symbol. Begin with the simple dog project shown below. Then check out books from the library for instructions for making more complicated origami projects.

Make a Dog
- *Fold a square piece of paper in half to form a triangle.*
- *Fold two of the points down to form ears.*
- *Paint a face on the front to finish the dog.*

UNLICENSED DRIVERS

Class Activity

Ask students to find out from which countries their ancestors came. Locate the countries on a world map. Then reproduce and distribute copies of the license plate on page 18. Have students decorate the license plate to tell about their family and the country from which they came. Brainstorm ideas for decorating, such as drawing a map or flag of the country, writing the country's name, writing your family's name, drawing picture of family members, and so forth.

Name _____

A Special License Plate

Cut out the license plate.

Decorate it in a way that tells something about your family's history.

Music Around the World

MAKE MUSIC YOUR OWN

Class Activity

Students may enjoy creating body music, which is an African musical tradition. Explain that to make this unique kind of music, students may clap their hands; slap their shoulders, sides, and thighs; click their tongues; stomp their feet; or tap their cheeks and mouths. Encourage creativity as students improvise rhythms.

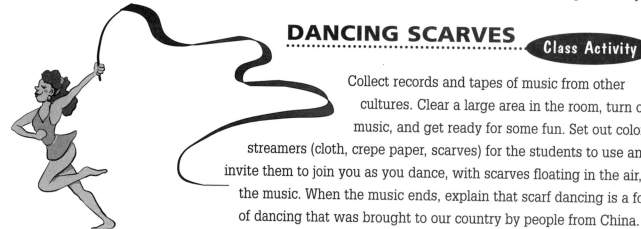

DANCING SCARVES

Class Activity

Collect records and tapes of music from other cultures. Clear a large area in the room, turn on the music, and get ready for some fun. Set out colorful streamers (cloth, crepe paper, scarves) for the students to use and invite them to join you as you dance, with scarves floating in the air, to the music. When the music ends, explain that scarf dancing is a form of dancing that was brought to our country by people from China.

MARIACHI BAND

Class Activity

Students may enjoy forming a Mexican mariachi band to perform for the class. The musicians stroll around the plaza, or room, as they play traditional instruments such as guitars, maracas, claves, drums. If you wish, you can have the students make homemade instruments.

	Description	Homemade Version
Guitars	stringed instrument	cardboard box with rubber bands
Maracas	gourd rattles	jars filled with beans
Claves	wood blocks	wooden unit blocks
Drums	percussion instrument	coffee cans with plastic lids

SOUND OF THE DISTANT DRUM

Class Activity

As you distribute copies of page 20, explain that drums are instruments that are used all over the world. Drums are used to accompany songs, to make their own music, and sometimes to send messages. Have students play the drum beats for a happy message and a sad message. Then challenge them to write a drum beat to show DANGER!

Name _____

Drum Talk

Tap the drum hard for every big X.

Tap the drum lightly for every little x.

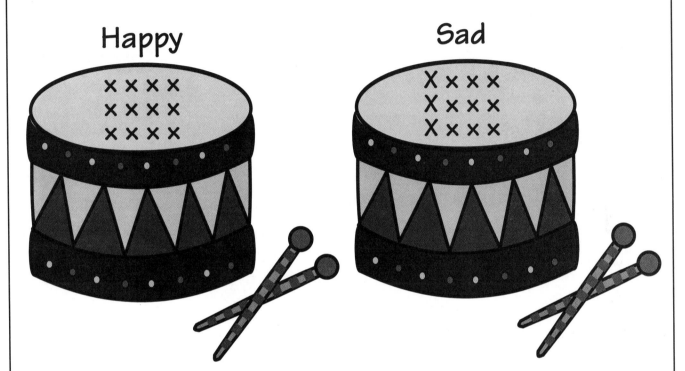

Happy

X X X X
X X X X
X X X X

Sad

X X X X
X X X X
X X X X

Danger

Write a drum
beat for Danger.

OLYMPIC IDEALS

Class Activity

Allow students to share in the spirit of the Olympics—peace, competition, friendship—as they learn about these ancient games. Let them know that every four years, the Olympic Games bring together the best athletes from around the world. The athletes come to compete against each other in many different sports and games.

OLYMPIC CREED

Class Activity

Explain to students that the Olympic Games began in Greece thousands of years ago. Point out that the Olympic Creed suggests that what is important is not whether you win or lose, but rather, that you participate. Ask students to tell what this might mean (to be a good sport and to compete to the best of your ability). Ask students if they agree with this and to explain their answers. Begin your plans for a class Olympics by writing a creed and posting it around the room.

CLASS OLYMPICS

Class Activity

Lead a discussion in which students determine the events that they will include in their class Olympics. In order to give everyone a chance to participate, allow students to select non-physical events, such as a spelling bee, geography bee, and so on, as well as physical events. Ask students to draw a separate symbol for each event. Provide ample time for students to practice the events before the competition begins. Record the results in each event on the reproducible chart on page 22 and celebrate with an awards ceremony at the conclusion of the Olympics.

OLYMPIC RINGS

Class Activity

Display a picture of the Olympic Rings. Explain that the circles represent the earth's six inhabited continents, and all the people of the world. Ask if anyone knows, or can guess, why the circles are locked together (to show the closeness or friendship of all the people in the world).

Set out small paper plates, crayons, scissors, and glue for students to make Olympic Rings. Suggest that students color the rims of the plates red, blue, yellow, black, and green. Rims cut apart from the plate can be glued together to make interlocking rings.

OLYMPIC MEDALS

Class Activity

Ask students if they know what kinds of awards are given to the top athletes at the Olympics (gold, silver, and bronze medals). Students may be interested to know that in the first Olympic Games, the prizes were wreaths made of plant leaves. Finally, help students make medals from foil-covered disks and striped ribbons.

FS-23221 Social Studies Made Simple ■ © Frank Schaffer Publications, Inc.

Olympic Games

Draw a picture for each game you will play.

Write the names of the winners.

Game	1st Place	2nd Place	3rd Place

A Beautiful Country

RIDDLE

Class Activity

Spark interest in the beauty of the world with this riddle.

> *From far away, I look blue and green. Up close, I have plains and valleys, hills and mountains, rivers and oceans, and deserts and forests that are filled with the colors of the rainbow. What am I?*
>
> (the Earth)

MURAL OF BEAUTY

Group Activity

Set aside ample time for students to share why they think America is such a beautiful country. Then organize the class into three cooperative groups. Assign each cooperative group a land or water form and have them cut pictures from magazines to show examples of their particular land or water form. Suggest that the groups finish by coming together to arrange and glue their pictures on a mural.

- Group 1: plains
- Group 2: hills and mountains
- Group 3: lakes, rivers, and oceans

KEEP AMERICA BEAUTIFUL

Class Activity

Ask students to pantomime ways that people can help to keep America clean. Then let students discuss, choose, and carry out one attention-getting idea that reminds people to keep their country clean. You may want to add a few school-based ideas to the list, such as painting garbage cans with the motto "KEEP AMERICA CLEAN," putting posters that say, "I LOVE TRASH!" on trash barrels, or presenting an award to recognize the beautification efforts of another class.

COLOR OF A GARDEN

Class Activity

Encourage students to add a little color to their world by planting a flower garden. Call a local plant nursery to find out which flowers grow best in your area and for advice on how best to plant the garden. You might want to select flowers that attract butterflies or birds.

SING OUT!

Class Activity

Distribute copies of the song on page 24 and have students sing it with you. Encourage students to tell what each line means. (Provide assistance with vocabulary as needed.) Invite students to underline their favorite line in the song and illustrate it with watercolors.

Sing Out!

Sing this favorite American tune.

America the Beautiful

Samuel Ward
Katherine Lee Bates

Reverently   C (I)   G$_7$(V$_7$)   C

1. O beau-ti-ful for spa-cious skies, For am-ber waves of grain,

G   D7   G7

For pur-ple moun-tain maj-es-ties A - bove the fruit-ed plain!

C   G7   C

A - mer - i -ca! A - mer - i -ca! God shed his grace on thee,

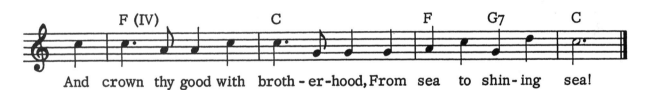

F (IV)   C   F   G7   C

And crown thy good with broth-er-hood, From sea to shin-ing sea!

Fifty Nifty States

Remind students that the United States is a very large country and that it is divided into smaller areas called states. Ask students to tell the number of states in the United States.

MY STATE

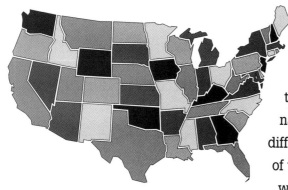

Provide the class with a jigsaw puzzle map of the United States to help them become familar with the shape of the nation and some of its states. Have students name their state and locate it on the puzzle map. Have students name special things about their state. If students have a difficult time getting started, ask about the weather, the location of the state in the United States, special events, famous people who live there, or favorite places to visit. Have them make awards that focus on the unique qualities of their state. Awards can be made with ribbon and tagboard.

STATE TREE

Display a picture of your state tree and help students identify it. If possible, take a walking field trip to find a living example of the tree. Ask students to take photographs of the tree or to draw it.

STATE POEM

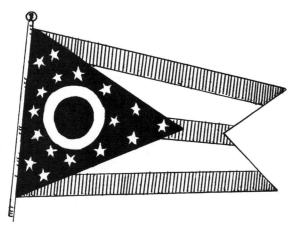

Students might enjoy writing acrostic poems about their state. Write the letters in the name of the state down the left side of their chalkboard. Then have students suggest words that begin with each letter that tell about their state. Here is what one seven-year-old boy wrote about Ohio.

O	*utrageous*
H	*ot*
I	*nteresting*
O	*ld*

STATE SYMBOLS

Go on a State Hunt. This activity is similar to a scavenger hunt, except that students are looking for information about their state. Copy and distribute the chart on page 26. Then, let small groups of students set out to find the necessary information. You may wish to assign an older student or adult to assist each group. For greater success, inform others around the school that they may be visited and what information they may be asked. Make sure information in reference books is clearly marked and easy to find.

FS-23221 Social Studies Made Simple ▪ © Frank Schaffer Publications, Inc.

State Hunt

Complete the chart.

Draw pictures or write words to show what you learn.

I Need to Find Out	Clue	What I Learned
Our state bird	Ask a 5th grader.	
Our state flower	Go to the media center. Ask for a picture.	
Our state flag	Go outside. Look on the flag pole.	
Our state nickname	Go to the library. Look in a book.	
A short way to write name of state	Go to the office. Look at an envelope.	

Parade of Presidents

Ask students to tell what these three people have in common: George Washington, Abraham Lincoln, and Bill Clinton (presidents of the United States).

WHITE HOUSE

Ask students if they know where the president lives? (in the White House in Washington, D.C.) Explain that when it was first built, the mansion was called the "President's Palace," but later, when it was painted white, people started calling it the White House. Have students look in books and magazines to find illustrations of the White House. Then have them draw their own versions of the White House. If some students are able to do so, ask them to design their own "White House."

WHO'S PRESIDENT NOW?

Have students make a quilt to tell about the current president of the United States. First, do some detective work to find out more about the president, such as:

- What is the president's name?
- How old is the president?
- How many children does the president have?
- What is the president's favorite food?
- What does the president like to do for fun?

Have a students' almanac and other reference books available to check facts. Then, have students color a quilt for the president using the reproducible pattern on page 28.

PRESIDENTIAL SEAL

Show pictures of the Seal of the President of the United States and explain that the seal is a large stamp or emblem that appears on many things the president uses, such as his desk, car, jet, and speaking podium. What do students see on the seal? Explain that the eagle is a symbol of the United States.

Cover 10" cardboard disks with aluminum foil. Have students use a blunt pencil to draw the Presidential Seal on their disk. Provide permanent markers so students can color their drawings.

Quilt for a President

Listen to your teacher's directions.

Then draw a quilt to tell about the president.

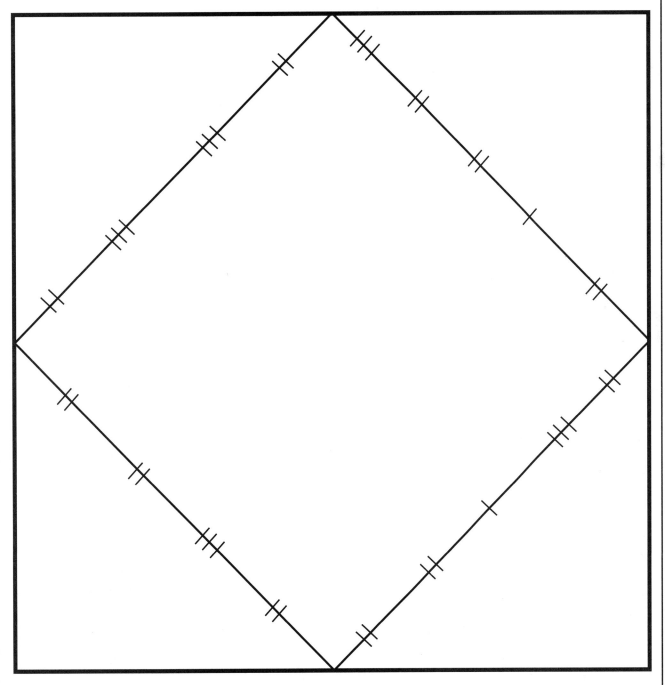

Pledge of Allegiance

WHAT DOES IT MEAN?

Explain that many Americans say the Pledge of Allegiance to the flag every day. Have students list on the board all of the places or events where they can remember saying the Pledge of Allegiance. Their list may include school, ballpark, soccer game or other sporting events, when you become a citizen of the United States, Fourth of July celebration, club meetings, and so on.

Students may have a difficult time understanding the vocabulary in the Pledge of Allegiance. To assist with understanding, write difficult words on the board. Help students find other words that mean about the same thing and write them beside the difficult words. Then challenge students to rewrite the Pledge of Allegiance in their own words. The following example is the way one young boy rewrote the pledge.

The Pledge of Allegiance
By Crockett

"I promise that I will be loyal to the flag of the United States of America and to the people and the government it stands for because this is a great nation with freedom and fairness for everyone."

MEMORIZE IT

Write the words to the Pledge of Allegiance on poster board and post it near the flag. Say the pledge over and over until students memorize the words. Invite young artists to decorate the poster in red, white, and blue.

SALUTE

Ask students to demonstrate how to stand when saluting the flag. Explain that most people stand tall and put their right hands over their hearts. There are other special ways that people salute the flag. Have students demonstrate each of these salutes:

Girl Scouts and Boy Scouts
Stand with 1, 2, or 3 fingers raised to the forehead.

People in Armed Forces
Stand with right hand raised to forehead.

People with hats or caps
Stand and place hat or cap over heart.

BETSY ROSS

Display pictures of the first United States flag (the flag of 1777) and the flag flown today. Have students compare the two flags. Distribute copies of page 30, inviting students to complete the drawing of our first flag.

FS-23221 Social Studies Made Simple ▪ © Frank Schaffer Publications, Inc.

Betsy Ross

Betsy Ross was a great American.

She may have created our first flag.

It was the first symbol of our country.

Color in this flag.

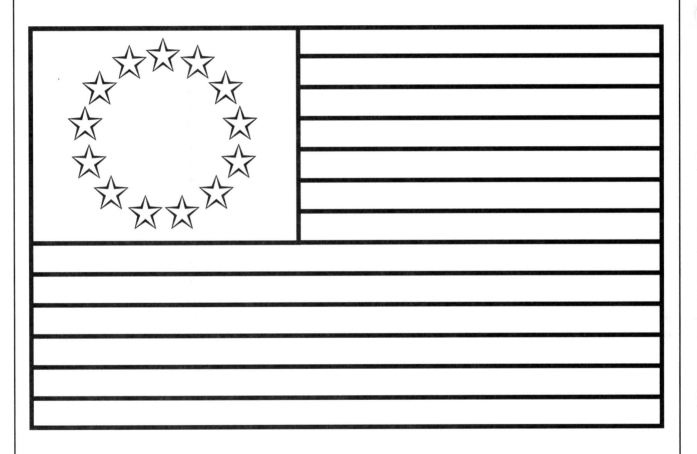

Independence Day

RIDDLE

Class Activity

Motivate interest in the subject by reading the following riddle to the class:

Q: What did the big firecracker say to the little firecracker?

A: My pop's bigger than your pop.

HAPPY BIRTHDAY!

Class Activity

Students may recall that Independence Day is the birthday of our country. It is celebrated on July 4. Ask students to pantomime activities that they do on Independence Day to celebrate. Some suggestions may be that they have a picnic, play games and sports, march in a parade, watch fireworks, play patriotic music, or wave a flag. Can others guess the actions?

FREEDOM RINGS!

Class Activity

Remind students that on this day, Americans celebrate their freedom. Look up the word *freedom* in the dictionary. Read the definition to students. Then work with students to rewrite the definition in student terms. Follow-up by hiding an alarm clock in the room. Set the clock to go off at different times throughout the day, marking the time for a "Freedom Rings" break. At each break, ask one student to share a freedom they have that makes them happy. Record the ideas in a class book.

PAINT IT!

Class Activity

Most students love fireworks. Celebrate the holiday with a classroom display. Give each student a piece of white construction paper. Instruct students to dip one end of a drinking straw into a container of tempera paint and to cover the other end with their thumbs. Then have each student dispense drops of paint onto the paper by holding the straw over the paper and releasing his or her thumb from the end of the straw. Repeat this process using a variety of colors. Next, have students use the drinking straws to blow the drops of paint around the paper. Some young artists may wish to add a sprinkle of glitter. The effect is a colorful fireworks display exploding in the air.

FOURTH OF JULY POEM

Class Activity

Distribute copies of page 32 and assist students as they write diamanté (diamond-shaped) holiday poems.

Line 1: Wow!

Line 2: Independence Day

Line 3: Boom! (2 more July 4th noises.)

Line 4: Parades (3 more things they might see.)

Line 5: Proud (2 more ways they feel about July 4th.)

Line 6: July 4th

Line 7: Fun!

FS-23221 Social Studies Made Simple ▪ © Frank Schaffer Publications, Inc.

Fourth of July Poem

Write a poem about Independence Day.

Your teacher will help.

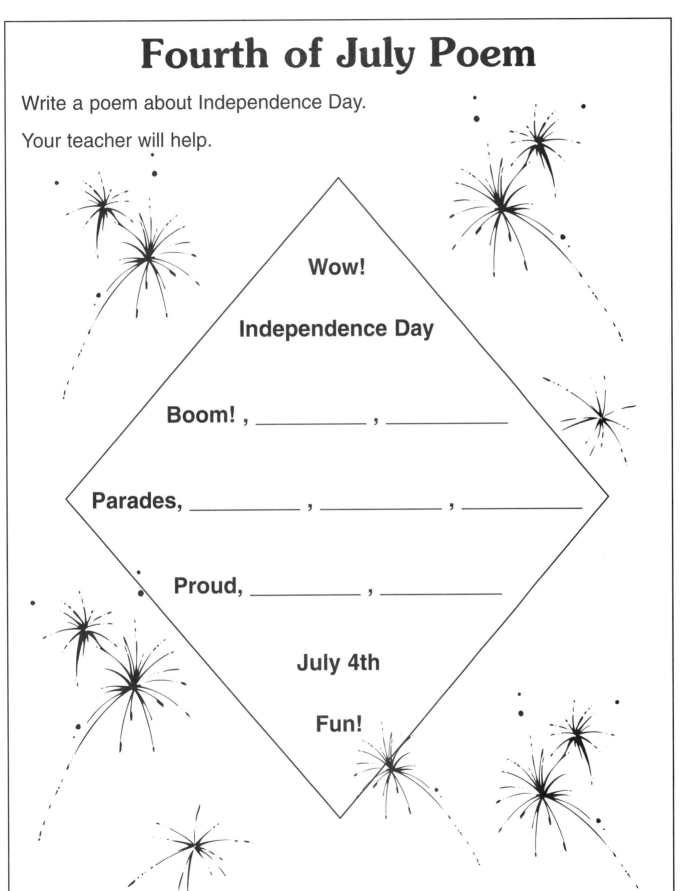

Wow!

Independence Day

Boom! , _____ , _____

Parades, _____ , _____ , _____

Proud, _____ , _____

July 4th

Fun!

School Maps

SYMBOLS

Take a walking trip around the classroom having students locate items which are normally kept out of clear view, such as extra books, paints and paintbrushes, lunchboxes, and paper towels. Together, create a picture to stand for each set of objects. Place the pictures near the real objects to mark their location. Ask how the pictures help find things. Point out that the pictures are symbols for the real things. Use the reproduction of page 34 to provide students with additional practice in developing symbols.

EGG MAP

Dye 12 hard-boiled eggs each a different color. To do this, dissolve food coloring in hot water and add a few drops of white vinegar. Display an egg carton with 12 colored eggs in it. Ask students to describe where specific eggs are. For example, a student might say that the blue egg is between two red eggs or the yellow egg is at the lower left end. Draw on the board a grid with 2 rows of 6 squares to resemble the egg carton. Challenge students to create a symbol to stand for the egg, perhaps a circle. Then invite students to use colored chalk to make a map of the eggs on the grid. Rearrange the eggs in the carton and revise the map.

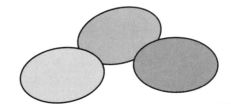

MAP A CENTER

Place a solid, light-color shower curtain and a box of assorted classroom materials (ruler, tape dispenser, book, pencil, hole punch, paper clip, etc.) on the floor. Have students arrange the materials on the shower curtain in any random fashion. Using marking pens, have students trace around the objects. Remove the objects. Discuss how the newly created "map" resembles the real center. Repeat the procedure using a different arrangement of objects.

CLASS MAP

Young map makers will enjoy creating maps of the classroom. First, decide on symbols to stand for desks, bookshelves, and other large objects in the room. Then let students draw the symbols on paper to show where each object is located in the room. Compare all of the maps. What things do they have in common? In what ways are they different?

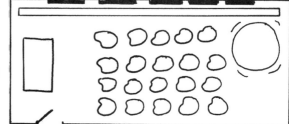

Name _____

Symbols and a Key

A map key tells you what the map symbols stand for.

Draw your own symbols for each of the things shown below.

Directions

WHICH WAY?

Class Activity

Students will enjoy using a compass to locate true north in the classroom. When this is accomplished, make a large sign that says "North" to mark that end of the room. Mark and add signs to identify the South, East, and West ends of the room, too.

TREASURE HUNT

Class Activity

Young treasure hunters will have fun following directions as they hunt for a special treat or treasure you have hidden in the room. Have students start at a designated spot in the room and follow your oral directions that gradually lead them to the treasure. Individual instructions should include the direction to travel and the number of steps.

PLAY A GAME

Class Activity

Invite pairs of students to play a game of Frogs in a Pond using reproducible page 36. Have the pairs sit back to back so they cannot see each other's gameboards. Instruct one student in each pair to color in the lilypads to show one path the frog could take to get to the flies. Remind students that the jumps are always forward and must be north, south, east, or west, but never diagonal. The same student then gives oral directions (north, south, east, west) to his or her partner so that their frog can take an identical path. After each direction, the partner colors the lilypad described before continuing. The partners do not look at each other's gameboards until the activity is complete, so they must rely on giving good, clear directions to follow the same path.

WEATHER VANE

Class Activity

Have students sit in a circle and pass around a weather vane. What do they notice about the vane? (Perhaps: It has a decorative piece; it has markers for north, south, east, west; it has an arrow.) Mount the weather vane in a clear place outdoors, having the directional markers pointing in the correct direction. Watch what happens when the wind blows. What did students learn about this weather instrument from performing this experiment?

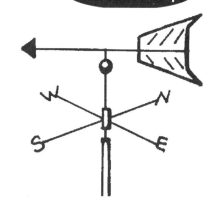

Name _____

Frogs in a Pond

This is a game for two people.

Your teacher will tell you how to play.

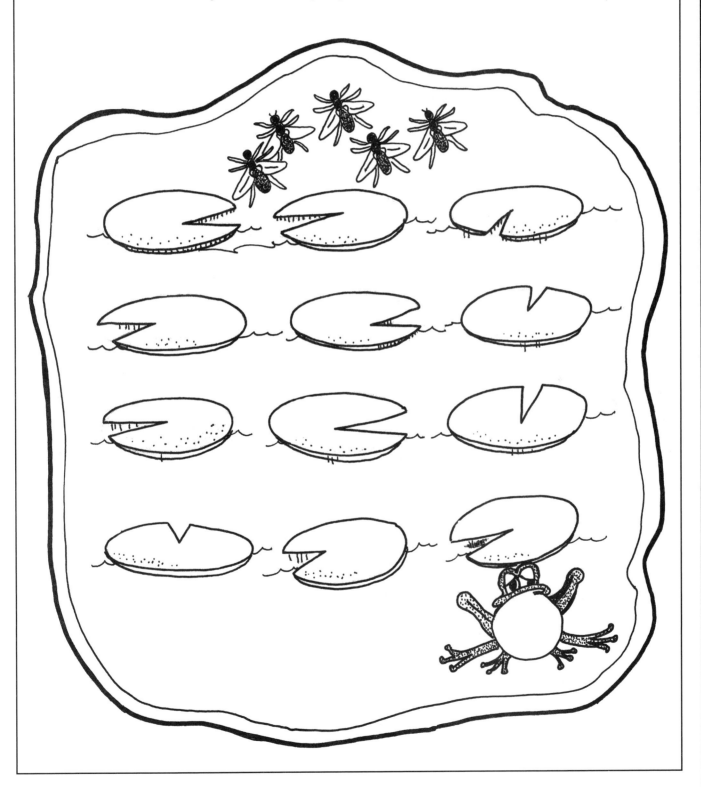

3-Dimensional Maps

SANDBOX MAP

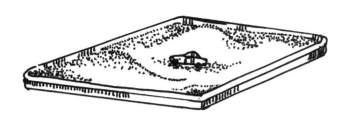

Set out cookie trays filled with damp sand and pass out wooden craft sticks. Have students sing "Over the Mountain." As they sing, ask them to create the scene in the sand. Many students will want to pile sand to make a mountain and dig a road for cars to travel around the mountain. Ask students to make a surprise on the other side of the mountain. Invite each student to share his or her work with at least one other person. Then have each student draw a map of his or her sand scene. Encourage them to create symbols to represent the important objects on his or her maps.

OVER THE MOUNTAIN

(Sing to the tune of "*The Bear Went Over the Mountain*")

The bear went over the mountain,
The bear went over the mountain,
The bear went over the mountain,
To see what he could see.

The people drove 'round the mountain,
The people drove 'round the mountain,
The people drove 'round the mountain,
To see what they could see.

MAKE A MAP

The map on page 38 shows two major roads and a map key. Using various sizes and shapes of buttons or coins, have students build part of a community by placing the objects on the map along the two main roads. They should select a different shaped or colored object for each of the buildings indicated in the key. Point out that they can place more than one grocery store, fire station, and so on on their map, but that they must use the same object for all similar buildings. After placing their objects on the map, have them trace around each one of them. Some students might want to add color to their maps. Remind them that they must provide a key to indicate what each of the objects on the map stands for.

FS-23221 Social Studies Made Simple ■ © Frank Schaffer Publications, Inc.

Map Maker

Use different objects to build a model.

Trace around each object.

Make a map key.

Poe

Main   Street

Avenue

Map Key _____

☐ Grocery Store   ☐ Library   ☐ School   ☐ Town Hall

☐ Fire Station   ☐ Post Office   ☐ Police Station   ☐ Office Building

Globes

THE EARTH'S SHAPE

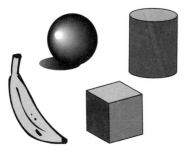

Display a variety of three-dimensional shapes such as an orange (or basketball), a banana, a box, a cylinder, a pyramid, etc. Ask students if they can think of other shapes that they have seen. Ask them to describe the shape of their classroom (square or rectangle) and their school (square or rectangle). Then ask them if they can describe the shape of the Earth. Which of the objects displayed is it shaped most similar to? Verify the shape of the Earth by displaying a globe.

CATCH IT!

Invite students to join you in a circle on the floor. Show them an inflatable globe (or make a replica from a blue balloon, coloring some areas dark green to resemble land masses). Toss the globe to a student. Ask that student to tell whether his or her right thumb (left pinkie, right pointer finger, etc.) is on land or water. How can you tell? (Green areas usually stand for land and blue is usually used to represent water.) Continue until all students have had more than one turn. Use this game at other in-between times, such as when lining up for lunch or waiting for morning announcements to begin.

GLOBAL DIRECTIONS

Point out to students the three most basic parts of a globe—the North Pole, the South Pole, and the Equator. Explain that the North Pole is the most northern place on the earth, and that the South Pole is the most southern place on the earth. Ask students to describe the relationship between the two poles and the Equator.

Have students write the words *north, south, east,* and *west* on a large beach ball. Then have them draw the equator around the center of the ball. Let students roll the ball back and forth to each other to observe that nothing on the globe itself moves; the equator is always halfway between the North Pole and South Pole and so on.

MAKE A GLOBE

Distribute copies of page 40 and read the directions with students. Assist them as needed in making papier-mâché globes. You may wish to use plaster strips available in school supply stores or art stores, which are easier to prepare than homemade newspaper and flour-paste papier-mâché.

Name _____

Make a Globe

Step 1
Blow up a balloon and tie it.

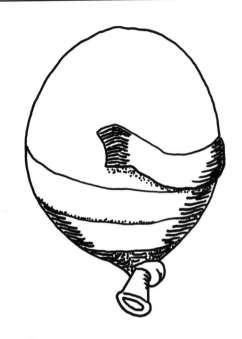

Step 2
Cover it with strips of papier-mâché.

Step 3
Let it dry.

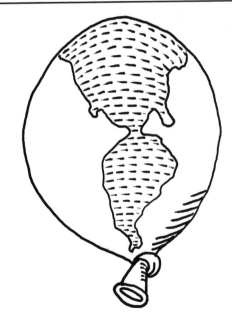

Step 4
Paint it.

Marvelous Maps

Maps can be fun when you use the techniques below to show students how we use maps in our everyday lives. Maps can help us to be safe, to grow a garden, or to understand where we live in relation to our neighbors.

FOLLOW A MAP

Class Activity

Students may have fun walking around the school, looking for different kinds of maps that people use. Keep an eye out for safety maps, such as escape routes in case of fire or other disasters and bus-loading maps. Study the fire escape map for your classroom. Then have a practice fire drill, following the directions on the map for exiting the building.

Fire alarm call point

GARDEN MAP

Class Activity

Help students plan a class garden. It might be an indoor garden in egg crates, a window garden, or an outdoor garden. In any event, it will require some discussion, thinking, and planning to decide what to plant, where to plant it, and how to tend it. Encourage young gardeners to make a map to show where each kind of seed will be planted in the garden. Then, divide the map into sections, asking individual students to be caretakers of that plot.

A STATE MAP

Class Activity

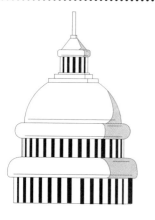

Remind students that our nation is divided into 50 parts called states. Ask them to name their state and the special city (state capital) where their state leaders work to make rules and laws for everyone in the state. Also ask them if they can name any of the states that border their state. Use page 42 as a vehicle for encouraging students to draw a map of their own state.

FS-23221 Social Studies Made Simple ■ © Frank Schaffer Publications, Inc.

State Map

Circle the state capital of New Jersey.

Underline the names of each of the states that touch New Jersey.

Trace over the Delaware River.

Color the Atlantic Ocean.

Wants and Needs

WANTS AND NEEDS

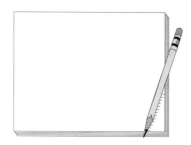

Ask each student to make a list of all the items he or she has in his or her bedroom at home. Discuss with them how their lives would have changed without each of these items. The goal is to determine which items they really must have (needs) and which items are nice-to-have luxuries (wants). Have each student categorize all items in a chart divided between needs and wants.

HANDS ACROSS THE WORLD

Help students understand that the United States buys goods from countries all around the world. Display several items that were built or grown in another country, such as toys from Taiwan, bananas from Costa Rica, winter coats from China, VCRs from Japan, and so on. Look for the words *Made in* _____ to help identify where the items came from and locate the places on a world map. Then suggest that students look for other items in the classroom that were made in countries other than the United States.

Made in China

Made in Taiwan

Made in USA Made in Japan in Costa Rica

ADS

Students will have fun creating their own ads for their favorite products. Talk about the most appealing characteristics of the products and why people like it. Then have students present their ads to the class. The ads might take the form of a commercial, song, poster, special packaging device, or some other attention-getting medium.

FUN FOOD

Invite students to name their favorite foods as you explain that food is something all people need. Then help them create a food chart using reproducible page 44. Have them cut out pictures from magazines and glue them into the appropriate spaces on the chart. Did they have any foods that did not fit in any space? Explain that some foods, such as potato chips and candy, are snacks. Students may want these foods from time to time, but they are not foods students need to stay healthy. Create a spot to put the pictures of Snack Foods.

Foods We Need

Cut out pictures of foods you like.

Glue these pictures on the chart.

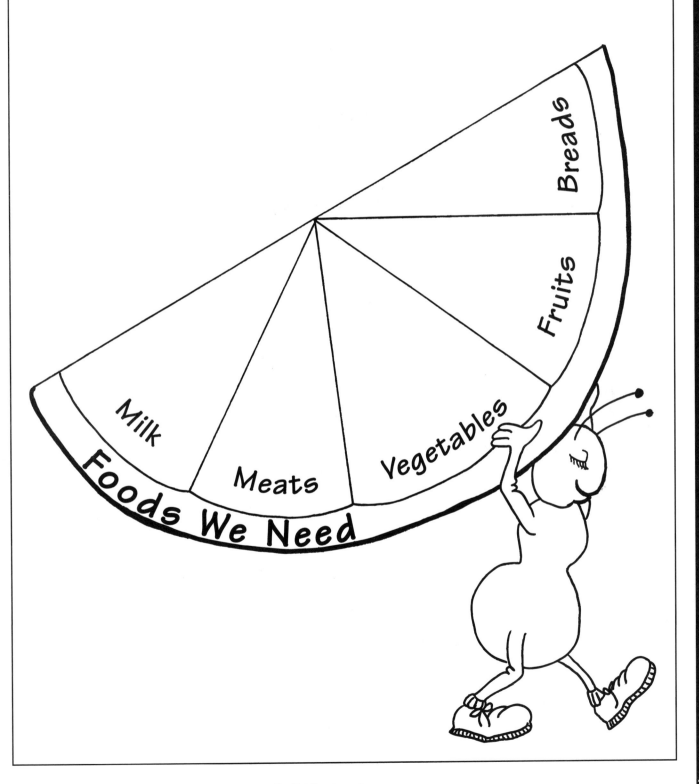

Community Workers

SERVICES AND GOODS

Have students name all the workers that they know in their community including family members and describe the work they think each worker does. Draw two large boxes on the chalkboard. Write the word *Services* in one box and the word *Goods* in the other. Explain that goods are things that people make or grow and that services are jobs that people do for others. Invite students to write the names of all the workers they suggested earlier in the appropriate box to show the kinds of work the workers do.

 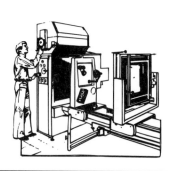  

POLICE ON DUTY

Invite students to role-play the jobs of different workers in their communities. To follow up, you might suggest a game to demonstrate one role of the police officer. Explain that this game is similar to "Red Light, Green Light." Have one student play the role of the police officer. The police officer should hold a sign in which one side is green with the word *GO* and the other side is red with the word *STOP*. All other students are motorists. To begin the game, the police officer holds up the GO sign and the motorists travel around the room, being careful not to crash into other motorists or structures. When the police officer shows the STOP sign, motorists must stop immediately. For added fun, the police officer may wish to issue traffic tickets to offenders.

SCAVENGER HUNT

Students will have fun collecting items to represent workers around their school. Organize the class into five small groups and assign an older student or parent to assist them.

Copy and distribute the list on page 46 for each group. Instruct each group to visit the school workers asking them for an item they use in their work. Put the items in a bag. When you return to the classroom, have each group share its items with the class, encouraging the students to guess which worker uses the item.

Name _____

Scavenger Hunt

Visit each person on the list below.

Ask each person for an item he or she uses in his or her work.

Draw a picture of what the person gave you.

Principal	Cook
Librarian	Custodian
Teacher	Nurse

Goods! Goods! Goods!

Remind students that people work to earn money so that they can buy things. The things we want and need are called goods. Workers make or grow these goods.

GOTTA HAVE IT!

Class Activity

Have students brainstorm an inexpensive item they want for the classroom, such as blocks, a book, or a new game. Discuss the merits of each item, including how it would be used, the cost, and why it is needed or wanted. Then have students vote on one item to purchase. (Guide students to select an item under $20.)

MAKE A PLAN

Group Activity

To reinforce the concept of earning money to buy things, suggest to students that they plant a garden. Let them harvest and sell the items they grow. Students should work in cooperative groups to prepare for the sale. Create a job chart and let students sign up for jobs such as advertising the sale, setting up the booth, pricing, delivering the goods, and collecting the money.

PROFIT PAD

Class Activity

Have students record the money received each day on a profit pad. Provide a calculator to add the running total. Have students color in the spaces on the graph to show the total amount earned each day.

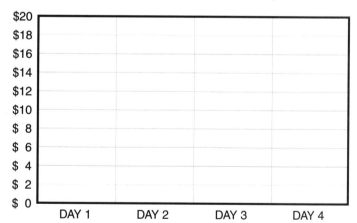

Profit Pad

Day 1 $ _____

Day 2 $ _____

Day 1 and 2 together $ _____

Day 3 $ _____

Days 1, 2, 3 together $ _____

Day 4 $ _____

Days 1, 2, 3, 4 together $ _____

MIX AND MATCH

Class Activity

Hold a contest for a design of a basketball uniform. Have each student design his or her own uniform and tell why others should buy that uniform. Students might create some special features for uniform components, e.g. sneakers with greater bounce in them. Finally, you might want to have students create an advertising poster intended to promote their uniform. You might wish to extend this activity to the design of other sports uniforms and/or play clothes, toys, etc.

Name _____

Design a Uniform

Design and color each of the items shown below.

Then tell class members why they should buy your uniform.

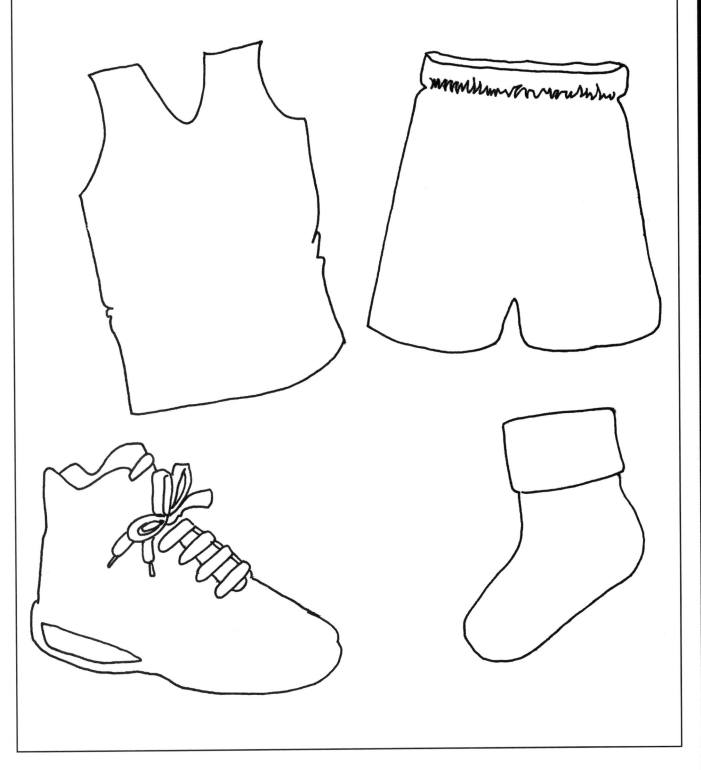

Fair Trade

BARTERING

Explain that long ago, people often traded, or bartered, things they made or grew for goods they wanted. For example, someone who grew corn might trade some of that corn to someone who made barrels. The barrel maker would provide the corn grower with barrels for the corn. Sometimes people provided goods such as corn or firewood to teachers as a way of paying the teachers for the service of teaching their children.

Invite interested students to act out the familiar fairy tale, *Jack and the Beanstalk*. What did Jack trade for the magic beans? Have students tell what they would have bartered for.

MONEY TRAVELS

Explain that before real money was made, many people used things like beads, beans, blocks of salt, shells, and small stones as money. Tell students that each country has its own money. Ask students to check with friends and relatives to see if they have any foreign coins. If so, students can ask if they may borrow the coins to bring in to show the class. Locate on the globe the country from which each of the coins came.

COLLECTING COINS

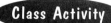

Invite a coin collector to share his or her collections with the class. This may encourage students to start their own collections. Tell students that someone who collects coins is called a *numismatist*. Challenge students to find a penny, a nickel, and a dime from the year they were born.

HOW COINS ARE MADE

Copy reproducible page 50 for each student. Read the page together. Then, have students lay Lincoln head pennies under their paper and color over the top of the paper with a pencil. Watch as the imprint appears. Ask students to complete the bottom of the page. Remind them that the faces of famous people often appear on the fronts of coins. Have students draw a new design for a penny using the picture of a famous person they know.

Spotlight: Designing Coins

Place a penny under this piece of paper with Lincoln's head up.

Then color over the top of the paper with a pencil.

Draw a design for a new penny. Show the front and the back.

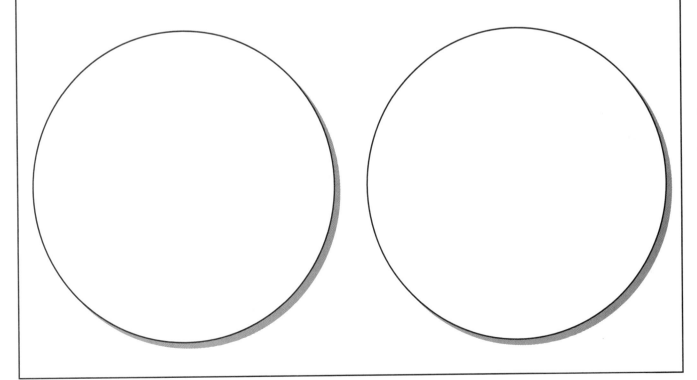

Inventions

WHY PEOPLE INVENT

Class Activity

Explain that people invent things for many reasons. Some people work on inventions in order to make money. Others do so because they are curious, or perhaps because there is a need for something new that will help them do a job better or faster. Whatever the reason, all inventors are creative people. Share some examples with the students and then encourage them to brainstorm other inventions they know about.

Inventor	Invention	Replaced	Need
William Addis	toothbrush	toothpick	cleans teeth better
Thomas Edison	electric light	candles	less messy, brighter light
Howard Aiken and others	computer	typewriter	faster, can do more, great memory storage

SOLVING A PROBLEM

Group Activity

Challenge students to become inventors. Explain that they should first think about a problem. Then, they must create something to solve the problem. For example, washing dirty socks out by hand will get them clean, but it is hard work, and it takes a long time. An inventor, Chester Stone, thought about the problem and then invented a machine that cleaned clothes in a tub of soapy water. Ask students to name the modern invention—the washing machine. Invite pairs of students to create new inventions that help solve a problem. The inventions may be presented as ideas, drawings, or models.

WACKY IDEAS FOR PETS

Class Activity

Students will chuckle at these wacky inventions. Write the chart on the board and then let students add other ideas for pets. Encourage creative thinking.

Problem	Solution	Who Solved Problem
bird made mess when flying around house	invented bird diaper	Bertha Dlugi
show dogs had dirty teeth	invented dog toothbrush	Bird Eyer
pets were not safe in car	invented pet car seat	Paul Rux

Students might be interested to know that the youngest inventor on record was only five years old! His name is Robert Patch, and he invented a special kind of toy truck in 1962.

FRISBEE RECORDS

Class Activity

Point out to students that the Frisbee was invented in 1968 and that Frisbee catching became so popular that there is a Frisbee competition for dogs! The world record for throwing a Frisbee is more than 623 feet for men and more than 410 feet for women. Use reproducible page 52 to have students graph how far each of them can throw a Frisbee.

Name _____

Frisbee Records

How far can you throw a Frisbee?

Throw it five times.

Record how far you threw it each time.

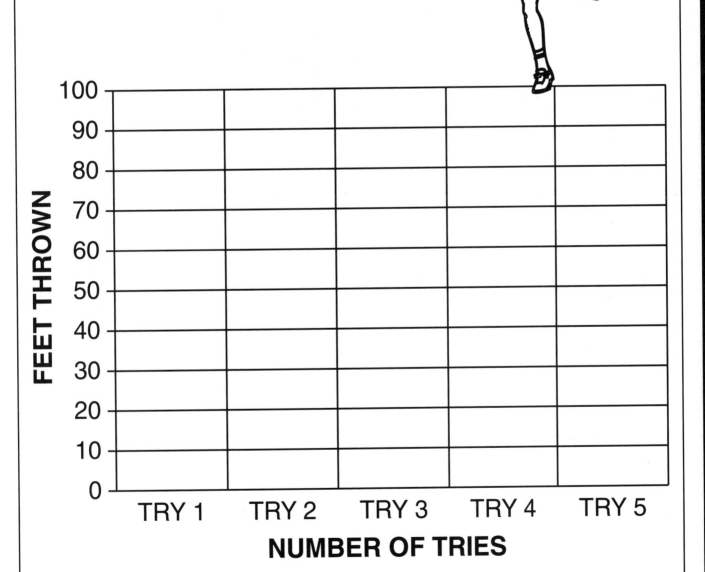

Selecting a Leader

FOLLOW THE LEADER

Play the game "Follow the Leader" with students. Pause a few minutes into the game and explain that you do not want to be the leader all the time. Challenge students to think of a fair way to choose the next leader. Traditionally in this game, the last person standing becomes the leader, but accept any reasonable alternative students decide upon. Continue playing until every student has had a chance to be the leader.

CLASSROOM LEADERS

Make a bulletin board that indicates specific classroom tasks that need to be done each day and assign students to assume responsibilities for those tasks on a rotating basis.

Use a chalkboard *If…Then* chart to help students think about the importance of being a leader and what might happen if the leader did a poor job.

If	*Then*
the leader doesn't know where to go	everyone will get lost
the leader runs	other people might run, too

SCHOOL LEADER

Do you have older students in your school who have been chosen to be leaders, such as safety patrols, tutors, student council officers, or hall monitors? Invite them to come to your class and tell the students what they had to do to become a leader and what their responsibilities are. This might be an excellent opportunity for students to tell student leaders about school rules they do not think are fair, asking why the policy is the way it is, and soliciting help for changing the rule if it needs to be.

LET'S VOTE ON IT!

Ask every student to suggest a class nickname. Narrow the choices to two. Next, distribute copies of reproducible page 54. Have students use the top of the page to make signs to campaign for the nickname they like best. Then help students record the two choices on the ballot at the bottom of the page and mark the nickname they want to vote for. Then place the ballots in a box in the room. Together, count the votes and announce the winning nickname.

FS-23221 Social Studies Made Simple ■ © Frank Schaffer Publications, Inc.

Name _____

Let's Vote on It!

Make a sign for your favorite nickname.

Then complete the ballot.

Your teacher will help you.

Vote!

Vote!

Vote!

Ballot

Nickname 1

☐ _____

Nickname 2

☐ _____

Laws

To reinforce the idea that laws are rules that everyone must follow, invite students to participate in the following activities.

CLASSROOM RULES

Class Activity

Ask students to create a list of rules that should be followed in their classroom, in their school, and on the school playground. Remind them to decide on a penalty for breaking any of these rules. Students with artistic talent might want to develop posters that indicate what the rules are and what the penalties are for breaking the rules.

PREDICTING CONSEQUENCES

Class Activity

Have students predict the consequences for breaking the rules. Begin by explaining that "predicting consequences" means carefully thinking about what might happen before we act. Copy the following chart on the board. Write one class rule above the chart. Then discuss with students the consequences of not following the rule. Follow the steps to decide if the consequences are reasonable and if the rule is justifiable. Repeat for other rules.

Predicting Consequences

Rule: _____

What might happen if we did not follow the rule? _____

What do you know that makes you think that could happen? _____

Based on what you know, do you think the prediction is likely? _____

Do you think the rule is reasonable? _____

BREAKING THE LAW

Class Activity

Discuss with students some laws that all citizens must obey every day such as traffic laws (e.g. speed limits), criminal laws (e.g. not taking other people's property), and civil laws (e.g. not trespassing on prohibited property). Invite a police officer or town official to speak to the class about the penalties for breaking such laws.

Use reproducible page 56 to help students classify various signs into two different categories.

Name _____

Sign Sense

Cut out the signs.

Put them under the correct heading.

Signs that tell you what to do.		Signs that tell you where things are.	

Democratic Behavior

DUCKS IN A POND

Class Activity

Invite students to join you in a circle on the floor. Explain to them that you are going to play a game called "Ducks in a Pond." Choose one player to be the Mother Duck. Explain that the other players are ducklings. Do not explain the rules. Instead, give the signal for the game to begin and walk away from the circle. After a few minutes, ask the students how they liked the game. Have them give examples of problems that arose. Ask if anyone has a suggestion for making the game more fun to play? Conclude by telling students that games are more fun to play when they have rules. See if this is true by having students play the game again, this time with rules. (The game is played in the same manner as "Duck, Duck, Goose," only in this version, the ducklings are chasing after their mother.)

NO PROBLEM!

Class Activity

When problems arise, help students talk them through and guide them as they work together to come up with the best idea for solving them. Start with the chart on page 58. Have one student state the problem. Then have the group brainstorm several possible ways to solve it. Look at each suggestion. Guide students to tell one good thing about the idea and one bad thing. Record all ideas. Then let students choose the best solution.

GOOD CITIZEN ALERT

Class Activity

Remind students that good citizens are people who are kind, obey the laws, and who help others in their community. Invite students to be on the lookout for good citizens, awarding the positive behavior by announcing to the class the student's name and good deed. Let students cut out and decorate GOOD CITIZEN vests from paper bags for the recognized students to wear for the day.

Directions for Making a Paper Bag Vest:
- *Pop out the sides of the bag and lay it flat*
- *Cut arms, neck, and front as shown.*

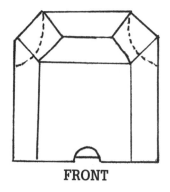

FRONT

BACK

No Problem!

Think about a problem you are having.

Use this chart to solve it.

Your teacher will help you.

Name _____

The problem is _____

Ideas that might solve the problem	Good thing(s) about the idea	Bad thing(s) about the idea
Idea Number 1		
Idea Number 2		
Idea Number 3		
Idea Number 4		
Idea Number 5		

The best solution is _____

Rights and Responsibilities

HELPING A FRIEND

Have students pretend that a relative of theirs has just come to the United States from another country and that the relative wants to become an American citizen. Ask students to write a letter to the relative giving that person information about citizenship in the United States that students believe is important.

IMPORTANT WORDS

Provide students with the following list of scrambled words. Ask them to unscramble the words and then use each word in a sentence, e.g. "The President lives in the White House. Our country is made up of 50 states."

tessta	states
wal	law
picatal	capital
dentipres	president
etihw esuoh	white house
ersdlea	leaders
erngovment	government

BROTHERHOOD BRACELETS

In the spirit of brotherhood, encourage students to show their friends that they care by making and trading Brotherhood Bracelets. To make the bracelets, children will need 7″ lengths of ultra-fine elastic and small beads in a variety of colors and shapes. Instruct children to create an interesting pattern when they string the beads on the elastic, by grouping different colors together.

DOING GOOD DEEDS

Ask students to request the help of their parents in clipping a newspaper article that tells about a local person who did a good deed to help someone else. Arrange the articles and pictures on a classroom bulletin board after students share them with the class. Read books about special Americans who did something good for their country.

DRAWING A STATE FLAG

Remind students about the four levels of government—local, county, state, and national. Every state government has its own unique flag. Display your state flag in the classroom, or provide students with illustrations of it. Use reproducible page 60 to have students draw their state flag. Also ask students to design their own state flags.

Drawing a State Flag

In the space below, draw and color in your state flag.

Now draw your own state flag.

Be sure to include in your flag symbols of things that you know about your state.

Ways to Get a Message Across

SIGNING

Do students know someone who is deaf? How do deaf people communicate? Many people who cannot hear use a special sign language with gestures and hand signals to communicate with others. Teach students to sign "I love you."

"I"

Hand touches chest.

"love"

Cross wrists over chest.

"you"

Index finger points at person you are talking about.

Invite someone to your class who knows the American Sign Language. Ask them to teach the students to sign a familiar song such as "Row, Row, Row Your Boat."

SHADOW PUPPETS

Shine a light on a light-colored wall or movie projector screen. Lead students to discover that when they block the light with their hands, they can form shadows on the wall. Ask students to tell stories using their hands to make shadow puppets. Have them write their stories on a piece of paper using symbols for each puppet or character.

FUN LANGUAGES

Have students share some of the words they use in place of *good* and *bad.* You may wish to explain that many groups of people have their own language. Truck drivers often talk to each other over a CB radio. Truck drivers have created a special language with words that mean something different to them than they do to most people. Share these CB words. Let students use them as they play the role of truck drivers talking to each other on CB radios.

Common Word or Phrase	CB Talk
get some sleep	cut some Zs
hear me	read me
O.K.	10-4
tunnel	hole in the wall
yes	Roger
return trip	flip side
location	10-20

911 CALLS

Set out two real (but not connected) or play telephones. Have students call 911 to report a make-believe emergency such as a fire or medical emergency. Play the role of the emergency operator, asking questions of the caller. Encourage students to practice using a calm, clear voice as they speak into the phone and to give this information:

- full name
- home address
- home phone number
- nature of emergency

FS-23221 Social Studies Made Simple ▪ © Frank Schaffer Publications, Inc.

Matchmaker

Cut out the cards.

Match pictures and ideas.

CUT

Stop.	Be quiet.		
O.K.	Hello.		
I don't know.	I'm cold.		

FS-23221 Social Studies Made Simple ■ © Frank Schaffer Publications, Inc.

Writing to Communicate Ideas

BALLOON MESSAGES

Class Activity

Explain that some messages can be conveyed in just one word, such as "Surprise!", "Fire!", and "Yes!" Ask students to add to the list of one-word messages. Organize the class into groups so that each group can be responsible for writing out one of the words on a series of balloons that they blow up. Each balloon should include one letter of the word being spelled out. Tie the balloons to a long string and stretch them across the room.

CUE CARDS

Class Activity

Put on a play about an event in our country's history such as the first Thanksgiving, the astronauts landing on the moon, or George Washington crossing the Delaware River. Invite the audience to play a part in the production by making sounds, such as clapping, stomping their feet, counting down, oohing, and cheering. Let volunteers print each audience direction in big letters on a cue card. During the play, have them hold up the cards at just the right time in the play and have the audience add the appropriate sound effects.

BUMPER STICKER

Class Activity

Discuss with students ways to make your community a better place to live. The ideas could include ways to clean up the environment, or suggestions for making a neighborhood safer. Help students create short slogans to express their ideas. Ask them to use permanent markers to write their short messages on strips of sticky-backed paper to make bumper stickers. Suggest that they get permission before attaching the bumper stickers to cars, wagons, or bikes.

WRITE A LETTER

Class Activity

Share this Will Rogers quote with students: "I never met a man I didn't like." Ask students to tell what the quote means to them. Encourage them to look for something good in each other and in every person they meet. Put every student's name into a box. Let each student pick a classmate's name from the box and tell something positive about that student. Follow up by having students write a letter to the classmate, naming characteristics that make them likable. You may wish to help students get started by reviewing letter format and copying a starter letter on the board for students to copy and complete.

PIN IT ON ME!

Class Activity

Communicate your ideas with wearable messages! Distribute reproducible page 64 and have students write messages about special events in your classroom on the buttons. Encourage them to wear the messages.

Pin It On Me!

Write a message on each button.

Cut out the buttons.

Pin them on.

Recording History

• Communication •

JOURNALS

Journals and Journeys

Color and cut out the cover.
Staple pages in the journal.
Write notes about daily life.

Journal

Read to the class a section from a biography of Christopher Columbus, George Washington, Neil Armstrong, Thomas Edison, Martin Luther King, Jr., or some other famous person who has made a significant contribution to American history. Then ask each student to pretend he or she is the person described in the reading. For example, some students might pretend to be Christopher Columbus making the long journey across the ocean to the "New World." Photocopy reproducible page 66 on heavy paper and distribute to students. Suggest that students write entries in the journal to tell what they see, hear, and feel.

TIME CAPSULE

Let students be a part of history! Ask them what they already know about time capsules. Explain that a time capsule is a container that is filled with keepsakes and information about you and the things you do every day. Invite students to make a time capsule to communicate with people in the future about their class. Have students think about the boys and girls that will be in first grade next year. What would your present students like next year's first-graders to know about their class? About you? About the music, foods, clothes, and TV shows they like? What would the class like next year's first-graders to know about special events and activities they did this year? Students might also want to write letters, make videotapes, and include photographs. Put all of the keepsakes into a container and save it for next year.

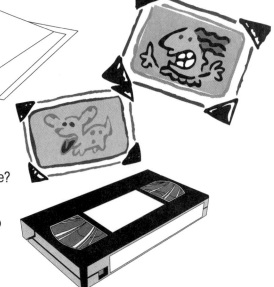

A BOOK ABOUT ME

Share a collection of easy to read autobiographies about famous people. Explain that an autobiography is a story of someone's life, written by that person. Students can record their own history by writing their own autobiography. Have them begin by collecting photos of themselves and gluing them into a scrapbook. Instruct them to write what they remember about each period of their life right on the scrapbook page with the corresponding photos. Encourage parents to assist students with this project.

Name _____

Journals and Journeys

Color and cut out the cover.

Staple pages in the journal.

Write notes about daily life.

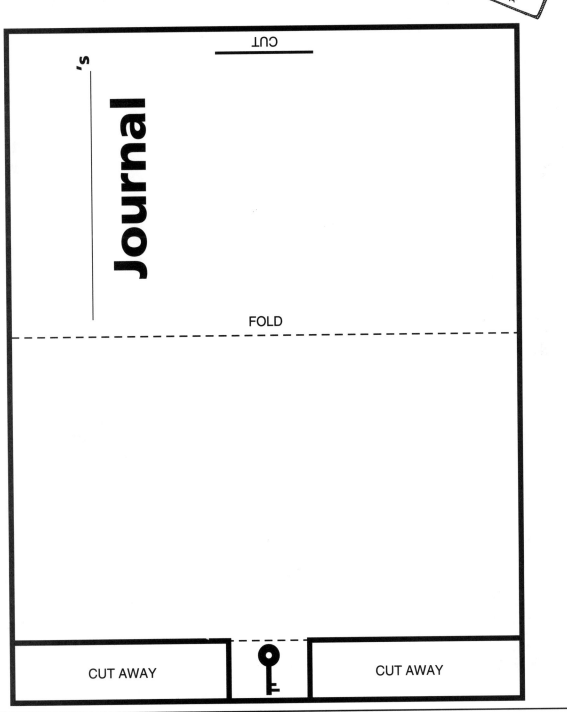

On Our Way

WAYS OF TRAVELING TO SCHOOL

How many different ways can students travel to get to school? Make a list of the suggestions. Point out some of the following unusual ways that students get to school.

Alaska	snowmobile
Figi Islands	boat
New York	subway
Japan	train
Africa	horse

Have students draw pictures of how they get to school. Also ask them to draw pictures of some of the more unusual ways that some students travel to school.

SING TRANSPORTATION SONGS

Discuss different ways to get from one place to another. Have students pantomime the mode they think of and let others guess it. Then, sing songs about transportation, including the following:

(From *Rise Up Singing*, 1992)
"The Wheels on the Bus"
"Riding In My Car"
"Yellow Submarine"

(From *Reader's Digest Students' Songbook,* 1985)
"Row, Row, Row Your Boat"
"Down by the Station"
"I've Been Working on the Railroad"

FLYING FUN

Set out model airplanes and let students demonstrate how they take off, fly, and land. Ask students to name parts of the plane they recognize, including the wings, engines, propellers, tail, landing gear, and so on. Help students make discoveries about airplanes and how they move.

What is it	Experiment	What Did You Learn
propeller	Watch how the wind moves a pinwheel.	The propeller pulls the plane forward.
jet engine	Blow up a ballon. Let it go. Watch how it moves.	The escaping air pushes the plane forward.

BUS SCHEDULE

Use the Dramatic Play center or a quiet corner of the room as a mock bus station. Provide chairs, a steering wheel, a driver's hat, a money box and coins, and other simple props. Have students take the roles of the bus driver and the riders as they pretend to travel on a bus. Use reproducible page 68 to have students create a bus schedule.

Name _____

Bus Schedule

Study the bus schedule. Fill in the missing time.

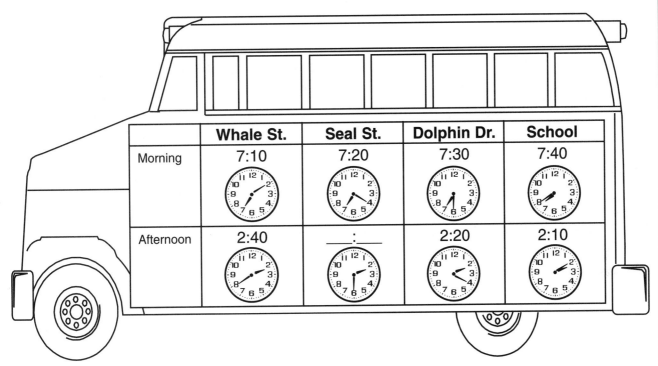

	Whale St.	Seal St.	Dolphin Dr.	School
Morning	7:10	7:20	7:30	7:40
Afternoon	2:40	__:__	2:20	2:10

Make your own bus schedule. Write in the street names where children will be picked up. Write in the times when the bus will reach each bus stop.

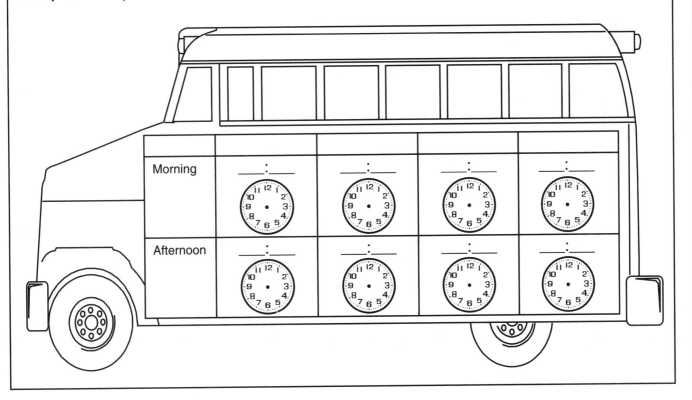

Morning	__:__	__:__	__:__	__:__
Afternoon	__:__	__:__	__:__	__:__

FS-23221 Social Studies Made Simple ▪ © Frank Schaffer Publications, Inc.

Goods to Market

CLIPS AND SNIPS

Class Activity

Discuss with students different methods of getting products to market. The list should include the following: car, bus, truck, boat or ship, horse, donkey, camel, elephant, train, airplane, and walking. Have students cut out pictures from old magazines that show products such as milk, food, clothing, furniture, toys, or other household items being taken to the market. Have students make a classroom bulletin board with the pictures.

DELIVERIES

Class Activity

Make arrangements to visit a grocery store to see delivery trucks as they unload produce and other products at the loading area of the store. To get the most from your trip, be sure to check with the store manager in advance to get permission and to select the day and time when several deliveries are scheduled to arrive. If possible, take the students into the store and watch as the products are stacked in the storeroom, priced, and placed on the store shelves.

SING A TRANSPORTING SONG

Class Activity

Sing the song "How People Get Bread" with the students. Then have them add actions to show the process of getting bread from the field to the family as suggested in the song.

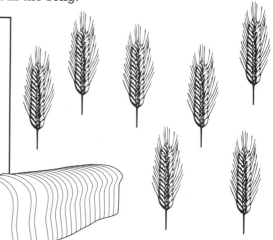

How People Get Bread
(Sing to the tune of "The Farmer in the Dell.")
Verse 1: **The farmer grows the wheat.**
　　　　　The farmer grows the wheat.
　　　　　Hi-ho the dairy-o,
　　　　　The farmer grows the wheat.
Verse 2: **The tractor cuts the wheat.**
Verse 3: **Trains take the wheat to mill.**
Verse 4: **Bakers make the bread.**
Verse 5: **Trucks take the bread to stores.**
Verse 6: **People buy the bread.**

CAPTAIN'S LOG

Class Activity

Distribute copies of page 70. As students look at the log, have them imagine that they are the captain of a ship. Explain that today, they will pick up a load in some faraway place and sail across the ocean to deliver it. Have them think about the trip before filling in the log. Students can draw pictures or write words on the log.

Captain's Log

A ship's captain must fill out the ship's log.

Pretend you are a ship's captain.

Fill in the log below.

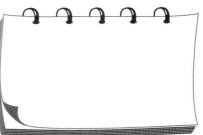

Captain's Log

Date: _____

Who is aboard? _____

_____

Today we will carry _____

_____

We will sail to _____

_____

Who will meet us at the dock? _____

_____

Tomorrow, we will pick up _____

_____

Signed,

_____

Captain

Using Animals for Transportation

HORSE HISTORY

Brainstorm a list of animals that are used to move people and goods from place to place. In the list, students will probably mention horses. Invite students who have had experiences riding a horse to share their adventures. Point out that for thousands of years horses have been useful animals. Once, they were the fastest way to travel on land. People trained wild horses to pull sleds, carts, and wagons, and to carry heavy loads on their backs.

Invite small groups of students to discuss why horses are no longer a popular means of transportation. Then have them draw an invention that lessened the need for horses. Have them clip the pictures to a clothesline strung across one corner of the room.

ELEPHANT POWER

Try this riddle with students to spark interest in the topic: I am the largest animal that lives on land. I may be taller than a classroom. I may weigh more than three cars. People sometimes ride on me. What am I? (an elephant)

Point out that elephants are used to carry large and heavy logs with their trunks. These logs can weigh as much as 600 pounds. Have students estimate how many students it would take to equal one 600-pound log. Have students weigh each other and add the weights with a calculator.

SLEDS, WAGONS, CARTS

Have students look in magazines and books for pictures of sleds, wagons, and carts that are pulled by animals. You might find pictures of rural areas in the world where dogs, donkeys, horses, reindeer, and oxen are used to pull heavy loads. Some students might want to find out more about dogsleds and how they are used. Explain that in parts of the world where snow and ice cover the ground most of the year, people travel in sleds pulled by dogs called huskies. Have volunteers locate

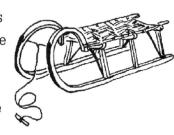

places on the map where dogsleds are used (Alaska, northwest Canada, Iceland, Greenland, Northern Russia, Lapland, and others). Point out that an Arctic sled dog is also called the Alaskan Malamute. Go on-line or use computer encyclopedias to find out more about this dog and why it is so popular with the Inuit.

Which Animal Would You Use?

Put a W beneath the animal you would use if you wanted to get somewhere in a hurry.

Put an X beneath the animal you would use to ride in a sandy area.

Put a Y beneath the animal you would use to pull a sled in the snow.

Put a Z beneath the animal you would use to carry a very heavy load.

Space Travel

SPACE GAME

Class Activity

Have students sit in a circle on the floor. Begin by naming something that goes into space. Then call on a student to name another vehicle that travels in space by counting down, "10-9-8-7-6-5-4-3-2-1-0, (student's name) turn!" Continue in this manner until students run out of ideas. A possible list might include rockets, probes, shuttle, satellites, missile, spacecraft, moon buggies, spaceship, space lab, lunar rover.

SPACE STATION *FREEDOM*

Class Activity

Tell students that a space station is a place where people can live and work in outer space. Add that NASA (a space agency) along with astronauts will be building the space station *Freedom* around the year 2000. It will have a sleeping area, a kitchen, and a workshop or lab. It might also have a stop-off place for rockets to land and get more fuel and supplies on the way to a distant planet. It could also have garages for rebuilding or repairing spacecrafts or storing lunar modules like the moon buggy. Have students suggest ideas for other additions to the space station *Freedom.* Then set out wooden blocks, making sure there are plenty of cylindrical and cone-shaped blocks, and invite students to build their own version of the space station *Freedom.*

BLAST OFF!

Class Activity

Ask students why they think people travel into outer space (to learn more about the Earth and the other planets, and to place satellites and other objects in space to help people on Earth get information quicker). Assist students as they make a model space shuttle using a toy airplane and three cardboard tubes (one for the fuel tank and two as booster rockets). Let students demonstrate how the space shuttle gets into space.

- Count down and lift off.
- Booster rockets lift the shuttle into space and then fall off.
- Shuttle runs off fuel tank while in space and then drops it.
- Shuttle lands on its own.

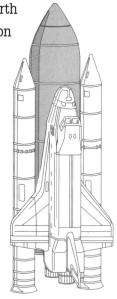

Name _____

Spacesuits

Look at the drawing below.

Label each of the following parts of the astronaut's spacesuit.

- helmet
- gloves
- backpack
- boots

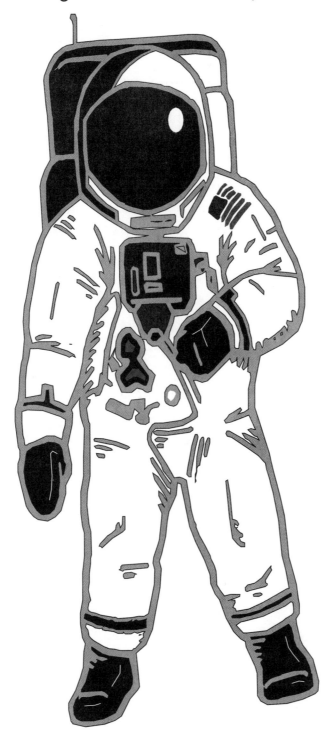

History of Transportation

Seven different ways of moving people and goods are shown below.

Number these items in the order in which you think they appeared.

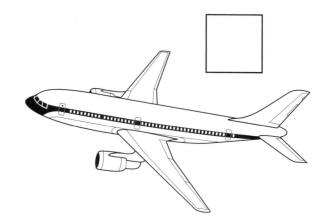

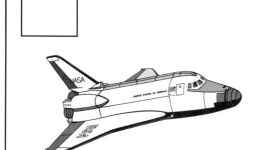

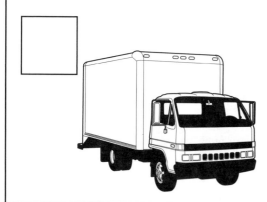

FS-23221 Social Studies Made Simple • © Frank Schaffer Publications, Inc.

Answer Key

Page 2

Answers will vary. Finished product should be a family tree with the names of family members on the acorns.

Page 4

Answers will vary. Finished newspapers should have headlines, pictures, and stories that describe some past event.

Page 6

Answers will vary but should include pictures of a quill, an ink pen, pencil, or marking pen.

Page 10

Puzzle pieces should be used to make a rabbit and a swan.

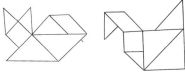

Page 12

food, airport (airplanes),

first aid, gas, telephone,

campground

Page 14

The finished product should be a decorated mask.

Page 18

Answers will vary. Finished license plates should show pertinent information about the origin of each student's family.

Page 20

Answers will vary but may include a pattern of big **X**'s to signal DANGER!

Page 22

Answers will vary. Finished chart should show 1st, 2nd, and 3rd place winners of class Olympics.

Page 26

Answers will vary. Completed chart should indicate name of state bird, state flower, state flag, state nickname, and abbreviation for state name.

Page 28

Answers will vary. Finished quilt should show pictures and pertinent information about the president of the United States.

Page 30

Finished product should show a colored-in version of the flag created by Betsy Ross with 13 stars and 13 stripes.

Page 32

Answers will vary. Finished product should be a poem about Independence Day.

Page 34

Answers will vary. Symbols drawn by students should be reflective of the real-life feature being symbolized.

Page 36

Answers will vary. Finished game should show path frogs took to get flies.

Page 38

Answers will vary. Finished map should show placement of all items indicated. These items should also be shown in the Map Key.

Page 40

Finished product is a papier-mâché globe.

Page 42

- Trenton should be circled.
- New York, Pennsylvania, and Delaware should be underlined.
- Delaware River should be traced.
- Atlantic Ocean should be colored.

Page 44

Answers will vary. Finished chart should include pictures of foods that correspond to the labels.

Page 46

Answers will vary. Students should draw pictures of objects used by different workers in the school.

Page 48

- Each set of uniforms should have a common color and design.
- Students should provide persuasive arguments for buying their uniforms.

Page 50

- Students should make rubbings of a penny.
- Answers will vary. Students should show their own designs for a new penny.

Page 52

Answers will vary. Graphs should show distances students throw Frisbees.

Page 54

- Students should make a sign for their favorite nicknames.
- Students should mark ballots to show name they will vote for.

Page 56

Signs that tell you what to do: traffic light, stop sign, no bikes allowed sign, pedestrian walk.

Signs that tell you where to go: restroom, gasoline, airport, first aid station.

Page 58

Answers will vary. Chart should show problem and five ideas for solving it as well as the pros and cons for each proposed solution.

Page 60

Students should draw and color their state flag. They should also create their own state flag based on their knowledge of the state.

Page 62

Stop.   Be quiet.   O.K.

Hello.   I don't know.   I'm cold.

Page 64

Answers will vary. Finished buttons should convey messages about special events.

Page 66

Answers will vary. Finished product should include entries about person selected for journal.

Page 68

- Seal Street Afternoon: 2:30
- Student Chart: Answers will vary. Finished product should show a real or make-believe bus schedule with streets and times indicated.

Page 70

Answers will vary. Finished log should include specific dates and products the captain will transport on his or her make-believe voyage.

Page 72

W underneath the horse

X underneath the camel

Y underneath the dog

Z underneath the elephant

Page 74

Students should label the following: helmet, backpack, boots, and gloves.

Page 75

Sequence should be: person walking; person riding a horse; ship; automobile; truck; airplane; space shuttle.

FS-23221 Social Studies Made Simple ■ © Frank Schaffer Publications, Inc.